PUERTO RICO

John Griffiths

Franklin Watts

London   New York   Sydney   Toronto

Facts al   co

Area:
8,897 sq. km.
(3,435 sq. miles)

Population:
3,435,000 (1987)

Capital:
San Juan

Largest Cities:
San Juan (429,000)
Bayamon (196,000)
Ponce (190,000)

Official languages:
Spanish and English

Religion:
Christianity

Main Exports:
Chemicals, petroleum
products, clothing,
machinery, fish, tobacco,
sugar

Currency:
U.S. Dollar

Franklin Watts
96 Leonard Street
London EC2A 4RH

Franklin Watts Inc.
387 Park Avenue South
New York, N.Y. 10016

ISBN: UK Edition 0 86313 966 3
ISBN: US Edition 0-531-10737-X
Library of Congress Catalog Card No:
89-8930

© Franklin Watts Limited 1989

Typeset by Lineage, Watford
Printed in Hong Kong

Maps: Simon Roulstone
Design: K & Co

Front Cover: ZEFA
Back Cover: Hutchinson Library

Photographs: Stephen Benson 5, 28; Anne
Bolt 15; The J Allan Cash Photolibrary
14, 31; J Griffiths 3, 12, 17, 26;
Hutchinson Library 18, 22; MacQuitty
International 23; David Simson 6, 8, 19,
21, 24, 25, 29, 30; Travel Photo
International 4, 13, 16, 27; ZEFA 7, 9,
20.

Stamps: Chris Fairclough

Puerto Rico is the easternmost of the four large islands which make up an island chain called the Greater Antilles. To the north is the Atlantic Ocean, to the south the Caribbean Sea. Puerto Rico's official name is the Commonwealth of Puerto Rico. All Puerto Ricans are citizens of the United States.

The land of Puerto Rico is varied. It has pleasant sandy beaches, and green mountain ranges and hills. Cacti grow on drier areas on the South Coast. The country is also well-known for its forest reserves.

The El Yunque rain forest, a short drive from the capital, San Juan, contains about 240 kinds of trees, including ancient cedars and satinwoods. The trees are covered in vines and orchids hang from their branches. The forest is also home to many kinds of tropical birds.

The Spaniards colonized Puerto Rico in 1508. They called it "The Land of Rivers". Parts of Puerto Rico are rainy. The mountain of El Yunque has 5100 mm (200 inches) of rain. The average rainfall in the north averages 1800 mm (71 inches) a year. Parts of the south coast have only 940 mm (37 inches).

Puerto Rico lies in the tropics, and average temperatures range between 23°C (73°F) in January and 27°C (81°F) in July. But cool trade winds, blow across the island from north to southwest and maintain a pleasant climate. Hurricanes sometimes strike the island.

In 1493, when Christopher Columbus visited the island, several groups of American Indian peoples lived there. Most were killed or died of European diseases. Today most Puerto Ricans are of Spanish descent. There are a few people of mixed Spanish and Indian descent and some blacks, the descendants of African slaves.

Puerto Rico became part of the United States after the Spanish-American War of 1898. In 1952, the country became the Commonwealth of Puerto Rico. The President of the United States is its Head of State. For that reason both countries' flags fly together.

The picture shows some stamps and money used in Puerto Rico. The main unit of currency is the United States dollar which is divided into 100 cents.

WORLD MAP

PUERTO RICO

Atlantic Ocean

Aguadilla

Arecibo

San Juan
Carolina

Culebra

Bayamón

Arecibo Observatory

Fajardo

PUERTO RICO

Mayagüez

Caguas

Central Mountains

Vieques

● Ponce

Caribbean Sea

11

San Juan, the capital, is a mixture of American-style high-rise hotels, and narrow streets and old Spanish buildings. It is Puerto Rico's main industrial and banking city.

12

Old San Juan is a walled city. Spanish houses of the 17th and 18th centuries have been restored. Many are now craft shops, small museums, and restaurants. To walk through the streets of Old San Juan is to walk through the Puerto Rico of long ago.

San Juan is the leading port, handling over three-quarters of Puerto Rico's foreign trade. Cruise ships, bringing mainly American tourists, are regular visitors to the port.

The Castle of El Morro in Old San Juan was built by the Spaniards in the 16th century. It was needed to protect San Juan from attacks by French and English buccaneers.

Ponce is a large city. It was named after Ponce de Leon who was the island's first Spanish Governor in 1508. It is the island's main port on the Caribbean Sea. Ponce is often called "the Pearl of the South", because of its many plazas, museums and public buildings.

Mayaguez is another port city. It was once called the needlework capital of Puerto Rico. The city has many fine Spanish buildings.

With help from the United States, Puerto Rico has become the most industrialized country in the Caribbean. Its industries include food processing, textiles, petro-chemicals, rum, medicines, metals and electrical and electronic assembly.

Farming is much less important in Puerto Rico than on many Caribbean Islands. Farmland covers 60 per cent of the land and milk, poultry and eggs are the most valuable products. Beef is also important. The main crops are sugarcane, tobacco, pineapples, coffee, and oranges.

Tourism is an important industry. Most of the 1.9 million tourists come from the United States, just 3½ hours by air from New York City. Tourists can exchange winter snow for the sun and beaches of the Caribbean.

Puerto Rico's future is closely linked to that of the United States. Most Caribbean and Latin American countries have fought for, and won, their independence. But in 1967, Puerto Ricans voted to maintain their ties with the United States.

The system of government is similar to that of a state in the United States. The Governor is elected by direct vote by the people for a four-year term. Members of the Senate and House of Representatives are elected for similar four-year periods.

The official languages are Spanish and English. Because of their close relationship with the United States, some Puerto Ricans fear that English will replace Spanish. They are worried that the newspapers, radio, and television are all in English.

Puerto Ricans enjoy many sports including athletics and many different ball games. Baseball and basketball have become very popular due to the influence of the United States.

The warm seas around the coast of Puerto Rico are ideal for many water sports. Surfing, swimming and sailing are popular. Many people enjoy deep-sea fishing for huge fish such as tuna and marlin.

Wood carving is the leading traditional craft in Puerto Rico. Puerto Rico's rain forests provide many valuable woods, such as mahogany, for carving.

Puerto Rico has three offshore islands: Mona to the west and Culebra and Vieques to the east. Ships sail from the port of Fajardo to Culebra and Vieques. The voyage lasts just an hour and a half but the sea can be extremely rough.

The Arecibo Observatory has the world's largest radio telescope. Opened in 1963, it is operated by Cornell University. It stands in a natural depression in the ground and its reflector is 305m (1,000 ft) across. The telescope is used to observe distant galaxies.

Although Puerto Rico no longer has any Indians, they have left many reminders of their presence. The Taino Ceremonial Ball Park stands where Indian chiefs celebrated rituals and took part in sports. Some say that the Tainos were the first to play baseball.

Education in Puerto Rico is like that in American schools. Sports, music and other social activities either come from, or are heavily influenced by, the United States. Puerto Rico is a crowded country and many young people want to move to the United States.

The Spanish brought Roman Catholicism to Puerto Rico. It is still the most important religion. Many North American churches have been set up in Puerto Rico in the 20th century. The Church of San Jose in San Juan was built in 1523.

Index